MW01088682

How to Get Your Wife to Cuckold You

A Couples Guide

By

Kat and Greg Webber

Contents

Introduction

You are probably wondering who we are and why we are writing this book, so we thought we would start there. We are Kat and Greg and we have been married for five years as of the writing of this book. To our friends and family, we have a normal monogamous relationship that is happy. We own a successful business together. Behind closed doors however, we have a cuckold relationship. We will make a few assumptions about your knowledge of the topic since you found this book. We expect that you at least have a general idea of what cuckolding is.

We are writing this book to help other couples who are interested in the lifestyle. We want to share our experiences with the world. Our relationship didn't start out this way, it evolved over time. We both read a lot about the topic as our relationship evolved. In particular, we enjoyed reading about other couple's experiences to help find our way through this new territory. Hearing about first-hand experiences on any topic you wish to learn about and explore is helpful. Now that we have settled into a comfortable place, we want to help others find their way.

The format of this book will be general information to start each chapter, followed by personal thoughts from both Kat and Greg individually. We hope this will give you the basic information plus a more personal spin that you can relate to. It is a well-known fact that men and women think differently about everything. Even if we agree on something, we usually have different reasons for thinking the way we do. By sharing not just general information, but also two different views of that information, we hope to really give you a great sense of the topics.

We should point out here that we are not "experts" in any real definition of the word. Neither of us have a PHD in psychology or anything like that. We are small business owners who happen to have a non-conventional marriage. So, this book is meant to be an anecdote. It is just our

experience and knowledge from living through this that we are sharing with you. If you truly want an expert opinion on the state of your marriage and how to improve, there are plenty of therapists willing to help. We would recommend one who is an expert in sex therapy. They will be familiar with any "non-conventional" relationship types and be comfortable talking about why you want your wife to cheat on you, or why you want your husband to watch you fuck another man.
 They also will be comfortable talking about any fetishes either of you might have.

Terminology

- Cuckold or Cucks – Husband of woman who sleeps with other men.

- Cuckoldress – Wife who sleeps with men other than her husband.

- BBC – Big Black Cock. A common fetish for a cuck to enjoy watching his wife with a black man whose cock is substantially bigger than the cucks.

- Beta Males – A term used to describe submissive men, especially if they are in a situation which emasculates them.

- Bull – The man who is fucking a cuck's wife. Often an alpha male type of guy.

- Candaulism – The practice or fantasy of a man revealing his female partner to others.

- Cuckqueen – Woman whose husband sleeps with other women, the reverse situation of a cuckold.

- Erotic Humiliation – Being sexually aroused from humiliation. A common fetish for cucks.

- Feminization or Sissification – A male behaving in a more feminine manner. This could include dressing like a woman, wearing makeup, nail polish, etc. Can also include mannerisms like tone of voice and posture. Also can include doing things thought of traditionally as female tasks, like cleaning or cooking.

- Pegging – The sexual act of a woman fucking a man anally with a strap-on dildo.

- Hotwife – A woman who sleeps with other men with the approval of her husband.

- Hotwifing – A man convincing his wife to sleep with another man.

- Monogamish – A couple who is perceived to be monogamous but are not 100% monogamous.

Types of Cuck Relationships

The "True" or Traditional Cuck

There is much debate in the community about what makes a "true" cuck. Typically, this is thought of as the man who is forced into a cuckolding relationship by his wife. This type of man finds out his wife is cheating on him, and finds he is aroused by the shame and the thought of her being fucked by someone else. Their relationship transforms from this place.

These couples tend to be a woman who is dominant in all or most aspects of the relationship and the male is submissive. The wife will often deny the husband sexual pleasure. She will often have sexual encounters with other men without her husband present or even without him knowing at all. What she tells him and includes him in is entirely up to her because she has 100% control. The man most certainly is enjoying the shame he feels in a masochistic way.

The Non-Traditional Cuck

These couples tend to get to a cuckolding relationship through open communication. Usually the husband suggests that he wants her to get involved with someone else. This can start as fantasy then progress to reality. The husband may or may not be present when the wife has sex with other men. If he is present, he may or may not be involved. But there is open communication. Often these cucks are aroused by their wives telling them the story of how another man fucked them.

The big differences here is there is no "cheating" and the partners are more equal outside the bedroom. The husband is often only sexually submissive, but treated as an equal in all other regards. The cuck enjoys his wife's sexual prowess and is usually desires her even more after she has been with another man.

The Fem or Sissy Cuck

This type of cuck enjoys feminization brought on by his wife. He might even enjoy "forced" feminization from his wife. He typically thinks of himself as inadequate to please his wife sexually and enjoys the humiliation of watching her fuck another man. This can also include him being aroused by hearing in graphic detail how the other man fucked her and gave her pleasure the husband could not.

This type of wife tends to be dominate in all aspects of the relationship like the "true" cuckolding relationship. She also will likely have sexual experiences with other men without any involvement of her husband.

This type of cuck is typically has some bi-sexual tendencies. He will typically enjoy his wife pegging (fucking him anally with a strap-on dildo) him. He might also perform sexual acts on the other man. Common examples would be sucking the other man's dick and letting the other man fuck him anally. This type of cuck would usually never have another man perform these acts on him though since he is submissive and the other man is usually dominant.

Kat reacts: I really don't like the notion that the only "true" cuck is the man forced into the situation by his cheating wife. I don't think it is healthy for a couple to live like that. Even if he "enjoys" it, it should be an open and honest situation. I know that some men enjoy having no control over the situation. But you can gain that feeling of having no power if you give your wife absolute say over who she sleeps with. She can also take control over if you get to be involved and if you do, now much you get to be involved.

Open communication is one of the most important factors in a happy and healthy marriage. I love having my husband watch me fuck other men. I love to tell him in graphic detail about things I do when he is not around. However, the thought of actually "cheating" on him in the true sense of the word makes me sick to my stomach. I love him and try very hard not to do anything that will hurt him.

I know there is much debate on this topic and at the end of the day, it is up to the individuals as to what works for them. If you want or have a "true" cuck relationship and you are both happy with the arrangement, then more power to you. Life is too short to not be happy. For me, I could not be happy deceiving my husband. Talking openly about everything is what works for us. Find what works for you and do it!

Greg reacts: I am more a firm believer in the "true" cuck than Kat. For me, the humiliation is a big part of it and that is more intense if forced. We all know that the term cuck has been became a popular insult with highest level of degradation. What the insult implies is that you are unwanted, undesired, and deemed inadequate beta male by your lover. You can thank the internet for that one, with the term being thrown about freely in the chats or message boards of reddit and voice coms of pretty much every online player vs player game.

But it didn't used to be that way. The term actually has a long history in medieval folklore, derived from Cuckoo bird that lays its eggs in other bird's nests. Usually it was used in literature of the time to satire a husband being deceived by his unfaithful wife and find out about it when she gives birth to someone else's child. DAMN!

You can even find cuckold in Shakespeare's work, with several of his characters suspecting that may have just become one. In western medieval traditions, cuckold was referred to as "wearing the horns of the cuckold'. What they meant by that is a reference to the mating habits of stags, who would forfeit their mates when they were defeated by a dominate. Some paintings from the 1800's show rooms filled with alpha men and a woman wearing the horns of her previous stag. The beta, usually cowering down in a kneel, his horns since removed. The assumption being his masculinity and the ability to retake his mate taken away from him.

But now, let's take this into the modern day and speak from my personal experience. When I'd browse porn on the web in the early 2000's, anything with Cuckold in the title of the video would just have a wife taking it from another man that had a bigger cock than her husbands. To me, these videos it just seemed like basic cheat porn. The husband wouldn't be around but the only context given was the male actor was bigger than her husband. Honestly back then, I wouldn't give it much thought other than that. Besides who cares, I was just there to rub one out.

But nowadays, this has been taken to extremes. With its growth in popularity, we start see gay actors playing husbands with their dick in cage watching from inches away while some hot porn-star wife sucks and fucks a comically huge black man's cock. All the while, the husband just looks pathetically from whatever vantage point as the wife gets pleased every which way by her bull. The wife will constantly insult the husband, comparing him to her 'better' lover.

Now with that being said, let's go through the many layers of cuckold; what situation is a cuck and what is not.

Having your wife jerk you off while she tells you about her *past* experiences with other men. While erotic as all hell, she's not cheating on you, therefore not a cuck. *NOTE: if you want your wife to cuck you, and don't know how to bring it up, this a GREAT place to start. More on that later.*

Knowingly sharing your wife with your friend, whether you are watching or not. Nope! Not a true cuck. That's hotwifing. It's not cheating, and she still sees you as her alpha. My wife and I sit around in this category with roleplaying that merges over into the next example.

Now let's say, you're watching your wife fuck your best friend and she says, "He's so much bigger." or "way better than (your name)'s" and she *means* it, congratulations! Now you're being truly cucked. She is experiencing another man's cock that she likes better than yours. The antlers have been removed from your head and now belong to your wife. You now have no control over the situation anymore and your wife will do whatever she wants, whomever she wants, whenever she wants. Now ask yourself, do you want that?

It's definitely not for everyone to be truly cucked, but some men love it. Feeling helpless, losing complete control while your wife gets off over and over because of her newfound authority. While it's definitely emotional masochism, some guys love the humiliation. If you have no qualms with that, and get off that your wife is now alpha, then cucking is for you.

Why cuck?

There are a couple of really obvious reasons here we will start with. One is that the husband enjoys the thought or reality of watching his wife fuck other men. The other is that the wife enjoys her husband watching her fuck other men. Likely the arrangement comes up because one of you is having repeated fantasies about this. It doesn't really matter who brings it up, now it is something you are considering. So why actually cross that line?

Maybe you have been married for a long time and are feeling that "7-year itch." That itch can come at any year really. You guys have fallen into a routine with sex and while it gets you off, it isn't anything like the excitement you both felt in the first few years. That is what started it for us. Well that is what drove Greg to bring it up. We were quite adventurous when dating and even had a few threesomes. Then we settled down a bit leading up to getting married and shortly thereafter got pregnant. A baby is a surefire way to take the spark out of the bedroom. But the time came that she got older and we rebuilt most of what we had lost. But we were still monogamous and had fallen into a routine. This lifestyle sure changed up our lives, bringing back the excitement that we had lost.

Or maybe you have been exploring the fantasy together and feel like it's not enough. For some couples, the fantasy is enough. The wife tells her husband detailed "stories" about fucking another man when really she went out and got a massage at the spa. Maybe she tells him how she fucked the masseuse! You guys have found that this it enough at first, but deep down you both know it's fantasy and it's not as exciting as it started out being. So, you want to ramp it up and actually cross that line.

If you haven't gotten to that stage, you might want to explore that for a bit first. There is a reason that many people say having a "threesome" always ruins a relationship. Although a "threesome" is different because usually all three people are involved equally. Bringing another person into the bedroom can cause a ton of problems. Even if it is casual and you don't really need to worry about the third person's emotions, it can cause unexpected jealousy and resentment. If you play with the same person repeatedly over a long period of time, emotions are more likely to come into play. It is harder than you think to maintain a long term casual relationship. More on that later.

The wife could feel pressured into crossing the line and end up having resentment. Or the husband could realize that while he loved the fantasy, reality is just too much and he feels jealousy. These feelings can cause long-term problems in the marriage. So you want to take your time and make sure that it is what you really want. This lifestyle isn't for everyone.

However, if it is for you, it will improve your marriage. Often the man feels much more desire for his wife after she has been with another man. The wife will often appreciate her husband more for the freedom she now has. It is likely to boost the woman's confidence, as she realizes there are men besides her husband that want her.

Communication will improve as this "secret" fantasy is no longer a secret. Sex between you two will likely change over time but it will become more fulfilling for you both as you are now talking openly about your fantasies and desires.

Prior to our marriage, Kat had explored her kinky side a lot but Greg was pretty vanilla. The transformation of our relationship has caused us to experiment more when it's just the two of us. This leads to us both being more satisfied with our sex life. Another added benefit is that Kat gets to pick men that are more kinky and explore things that Greg doesn't enjoy.

Overall, if it works for you, it will improve your relationship. Everyone's results will be different of course. But you will experience a new closeness and a renewed desire for each other. You will also come to appreciate each other more.

Kat reacts: This or any "non-traditional" relationship is not for everyone. I have had very few traditional relationships over the years so I was much more open to this whole idea than many wives would be. Nearly all my relationships have been monogamish or fully open. Even my relationship with Greg didn't start out as traditional. It ended up that way for many years before we started down the road to this lifestyle.

For me, the why should be that you both like the idea and think it will make you both happier. That is the best reason to make any decision really. Greg and I are a great team and we make decisions based on what will make us happiest. We make compromises and love our life. No matter what the reason you started reading this book, I hope it helps you find what will work for you.

Greg reacts: What can say? I like not being in control. I've always been a reserved person and my first sexual experience I had no clue what I was doing so the girl got frustrated, took control, and straddled me. This reluctance to take control of the situation plagued me for the first year or two of my sex life. I loved getting fucked while I laid there doing nothing. My first few girlfriends grew tired of it rather quickly and while I got better through experience, this overarching theme of not being the 'shot caller' during sex was always there.

Those first few years, I was called everything from lousy fuck, minuteman, but most of all - tiny dick. While I was defensive when being called these things in my immaturity, they were right. Oddly enough though, I made up for it with being funny and never had a shortage of girls that wanted to fuck. When I was in college, I joked my way into plenty of panties. It was when my pants came off the serious laughter started. While I was never turned down from sex, it was obvious by the tales they told their friends afterwards that they weren't in the least satisfied. Word spread quickly and the ridicule followed. This constant insulting from the opposite sex was hurtful at the beginning, but then it just turned into an everyday thing and became normal, making me desensitized. I tried everything to increase my size, pills at first then even penis pumps. But that ended when I got my cock stuck in one and had to take an embarrassing trip to an emergency room.

As time went on and I began to mature, the girls became women and my size didn't matter much anymore. I met Kat during this time. She had frequented clubs in the kink scene, specifically the ones where fem-domme was prominent. We were instantly a good pair. I learned so much about being a submissive during our first year together. While I don't like stereotypical kink that she was used to, I didn't hate it either. But it did open me up to sex in a nontraditional sense. In a strange way, it was kinda what I was used to. Except now, the embarrassing treatment happened before I got off which was a much better situation for me emotionally in my sex life.

So why other men?

Well, I'm addicted to pornography in all of its forms. When it comes to visual, I love watching petite girls getting banged by massive cocks. I liked being immersed in the fantasy that I was actually able to pleasure a woman like these porn-stars could. As far as written erotica, I preferred stories of cheating and hotwifing. But most of I loved it when I overheard ladies talking about their sex lives in explicit detail. Every time I was around when a female talked aloud about how some other man pleasured her, I was enthralled. My cock would come to life in my pants and I would leave to find a private place to rub one out.

I finally brought myself to ask my wife one day to tell me a story about one her past boyfriend's. Since she had a history in the kink scene she more than comfortable and open to. At first, she would tell me stories about her first sexual experiences whom happened to be with a guy named Roger. Just so happened that Roger had an enormous cock. And when I imagined my wife's pussy getting filled up by a large cock, I had to run in the bathroom and jerk off. She followed me in there once and caught me in the act. I was embarrassed at first, but she quickly calmed me down, telling me to carry on and continued her story about how his cock was so big that she came almost instantly when he stuck it in. I remember cumming so hard; and I'm not joking when I write this: my cum hit the ceiling.

I was so turned this that it actually started to become a part of our foreplay. I'd start asking for her to tell me more stories about Roger and how he was able to satisfy her while she jerked me off. I would cum so intensely every time I thought about her stories with this man. I could tell that Kat was getting worked up in storytelling as well, her stories became more erotic and vivid. She would get off furiously during this period of our sex life. I had a feeling by how her face was flushed with arousal that she was more getting off on the memory of this other man's cock than the one I was providing physically. Turned out, that my intuition was true.

I wished I was him, but I knew I'd never be him or even match up to him in the bedroom. This was something that I accepted. At the same time, I got me all sorts of worked up knowing that my wife was enjoying the stories as much as I did. I wanted her to be pleasured like that again. And one time when I was immersed in the fantasy of him banging my wife, the words slipped out of mouth mid orgasm- "I want to watch you getting fucked by Roger."

Starting the Conversation

The best way to bring about any change in a marriage, is to talk openly about it, slowly. Drastic change is hard for everyone. It doesn't matter if you are trying to lose weight, quit smoking, or change your marriage. We are all creatures of habit and find change scary at some level. This is not a change that you can make overnight. And we wouldn't even suggest you bring it all up at once.

Many women will freak out when their husband tells them that they want to watch her fuck another man. They will feel overwhelmed and wonder what his real motives are. Does he want to be able to fuck other women is the most common reaction from wives that don't see it coming. This is why it should be a gradual conversation.

There are other books out there that suggest methods over bringing this up to your wife that are borderline, if not downright, deceitful. That is not a healthy way to go about it. The key here is open and honest conversation at every stage along the way. So, start small, since it is likely you are a husband wanting to get your wife to cuck you, we will talk from that point of view but it could easily be reversed.

Ask her to tell you some naughty stories about her sexual experiences with other men as foreplay. This will help create an atmosphere where she is more comfortable talking about sex with other men to you. If you think even that is a little far stretched for your wife then maybe ask her about fantasies with her favorite movie star. The key here is to start the conversation.

Porn can be a great way to also get the idea brought up. Watching some mild cuck porn or even just threesome (MMF) porn together can get the conversation going. This really depends on if your wife enjoys watching porn. If she doesn't enjoy it, then talking is the better way to go.

Then you can work towards telling her that you enjoy the thought of watching her with another man. That situation you created when getting her to tell stories about the past now transforms into talking about the future. How exactly you do this will depend on how she is reacting, just take baby steps.

You could start with getting her to tell you a naughty story about her favorite musician. You two get backstage passes and he comes onto her. You totally play along like you are just a friend and watch. Talking about a hypothetical situation like has practically no chance of happening will be easier for her at first than talking about banging the pool boy. Keep that in mind, slowly work from "never going to happen" to "this might happen."

This could take months so be patient, it is a unique journey for everyone. Eventually work up to the point where you are now talking about her fucking John from the office or your buddy Tom. Oh, and keep in mind here, just because you know Tom thinks she is hot and would totally be willing to fuck her in front of you, does not mean she will have an interest in Tom.

Kat reacts: I have a read a few books that suggest manners of convincing your wife which I view as dishonest. I would seriously suggest that if you have gotten advice like that, ignore it! Sure, manipulating her MIGHT move the situation along more quickly or get her to do something she really doesn't want to do. But, when she finds out, she will be pissed. You want this to be an ongoing situation, right? I mean, if you were just after I one I time thing then you could go get drunk at a bar and find some guy willing to have a threesome. You are reading this book because you want more than a drunken one-time thing.

The only way you are going to get a long-term situation that you are both happy with, is open honest communication. Take your time, don't scare her, but don't lie either. How many years have you been married? Five? Ten? You want this situation to be going on in five more? Ten more? Then take a year or however long it takes to transform your lives. Yes, this might be mostly about sex and desires, but it also about your marriage being shaped in the way that makes you both the happiest. Sex, communication, and trust are the biggest factors to a happy marriage. Don't risk trust or communication for the sake of sex.

Greg reacts: All women are different and I got lucky with my wife being as open as she is. As continuing from last react, I worked it into story telling which converted into foreplay. This developed over time naturally with it finally asking her to let me watch her fuck one her ex boyfriends.

One thing I'd like to hit on, is that once you finally put it out there that you want her to fuck another man while you watch. There's no going back from this. Own your choice and know that it is going to satisfy you both. Which is why it's good to experiment with storytelling during foreplay and see how hard the both of you get off before bringing in another man. If you and your wife are peaking to orgasm faster than you normally would, then you're ready. Bring on the bull.

Turning Suggestions into Action

So, you guys have been playing out these what-if's and talking about the idea but the fantasy isn't enough for one or both of you. Time to cross that line! We would seriously suggest that the woman takes the lead here. As the husband, you can make the suggestion and let her know you really want it, but remember she is the one who is going to actually fuck someone else. Remember that, especially if she has not been with another partner in a very long time.

Women are usually very self-conscious and this whole thing is likely new territory for her. The last thing you want is for her to feel pressured and to regret what she did. It is likely she is going to feel more comfortable if you don't actually watch the first time. She might also want to explore slowly with a guy she chooses, not just jump right into bed with

him. Your best bet is to go at her pace.
Women vary dramatically at how they want
to proceed with the first encounter.

There really is no right or wrong way.
You simply need to come up with a plan that
you are both happy with. And guys, you want
to be more submissive and let her take more
control, now is the time! Compromise here so
you both feel like you are taking action at a
pace that you are happy about. Maybe the
wife just wants to be brave enough to make
out with some guy in a bar at first but nothing
more. Or maybe she has an ex-boyfriend that
she can resume fucking. Whatever works for
you guys, go with it. Take it as fast or as slow
as you are both comfortable.

Kat reacts: I got lucky in that I had an
ex who was single that I could easily sort of
rekindle things with. I made it clear to Roger
that I just wanted a 'friends with benefits'
type of thing and he was totally okay with

that. Greg did a great job of telling that story below so I won't rehash too much. Just say that this is a really critical time to let the wife have full control and set the pace. Too much pressure at this point can make a lot of women change their minds about actually crossing that line.

Greg reacts: For me, our first 'Bull' was an ex-boyfriend that she was comfortable with. She tracked down Roger on social media and started saying hello every now and then. I would ask her seldomly if she had messaged him but then in turned into a weekly status report. Things got friendly quickly between them because he just happened to be single and she was flirty. As she eased into him, she let him into the picture, telling Roger that she had told me about that 'one time'. He didn't think much of it at the time because she didn't tell him about my reaction to it. She saved that for a little later. But it did open their conversation and flirtiness into the sexual realm that involved my knowledge.

When I reviewed the chat log it seemed that he was more concerned with flirting with her after this point, rekindling from a romance they had long ago, not too concerned that his actions may cause an affair. Was he going to have animosity towards me like I wasn't treating her right and swoop in and try to snatch her away? Actually no, I lucked out, it was pretty obvious that Roger just wanted to get laid. And I was all about it! But was he ok with me knowing? Oddly enough, yep! Totally fine. She brought it up as a joke at first to toy with the idea and he replied, "I don't care if he knows." It bizarre how casual it all was looking back at it.

The flirting carried on for a month when Kat had messaged him and said that she would be in his area. She asked him to meet him for a drink, he agreed and she drove her car the 60 or so miles to the town he lived in. I told her I wanted to go but it was really already awkward enough and that she wouldn't be able to go through with it knowing I was creeping about. While I playfully accepted with an "Awe!", it took a lot to not follow her. But I respected her wishes and let her have a night out.

I was glad I did. When she returned she told me a story of how they met at some dive and got wasted. They got caught up with each other and as the night carried on the and drinks flowed they began to get touchy with each other. With her reservations gone from the booze she told him that she had only came to town to see him. Needless to say, they quickly took a cab back to his apartment and hooked up. I was so excited when she went over the details that we immediately fucked. I even had a double orgasm that night.

Two weekends later, they set up another date. But this time, I insisted that go and watch. Kat agreed but only from a distance. We drove separate cars and she met him at the same dive and I sat in my car in a dark spot in the parking lot. They must have had too many when they came out for their taxi because they were all over each other. Most men would have been completely shocked but not me. Besides it was my idea. I followed their cab to his place, Roger was too drunk to notice. They went inside and did their thing while rubbed one out in my car. I went and got a motel and waited for her call the next morning. When the call came in, I actually went and picked her up from his place. Which was a good sign, because now it was obvious that I was ok with her fucking other men. After speaking to him later about it, he was apprehensive until I actually picked her up. Roger had thought that Kat wasn't being truthful about the situation and that she had said that I knew just to calm his nerves. Don't blame him, I would have thought it was a lie too if it was any other lady.

With Kat's permission, I added Roger to my social media the next day, he accepted. I pleasantly invited him over. I still look at the message I sent him and laugh. I was straight and to the point. "Hey man, got a new big screen and watching the game this weekend. I'll let you come over and bone my wife if you bring the beer." And he did. Even asked me for my favorite brand, which brought over in copious amounts.

It just all worked itself out. He came over, we all cracked open some beers in the back yard and shot the shit. This was a critical moment. If I would have shown any reservations or apprehension on my face when I met Roger, it would've all been over. Kat was quick to take to a tequila bottle and play music. Before we knew we were having a good time getting to know each other while Kat was sure to give us both attention. Eventually she got tipsy and couldn't control herself anymore. She started sitting close to him and rubbing his thigh. I just sat there like nothing was wrong at first but I could tell it was awkward for him. So, I decided to pipe up with "Kat, your hand is not close enough." We all laughed as her hand moved closer to his cock and began rubbing him through his pants. This persisted and one thing led to another and before I knew it she was giving Roger head while I watched. To this day, it was one of the most erotic things I've ever witnessed.

Common Fetishes

Obviously, there is a countless number of fetishes out in the world. Just about anything you can think up, someone is turned on by it. There are some common fetishes though to the cuckold world. However, it is worth noting that everyone is different and all cuck relationships are different. Some of you will probably only enjoy one or two things on this list. Some of you might enjoy them all. There is no right or wrong way, we just list things here that are common. They are also things you will commonly see in porn that is labeled as cuck.

Probably the most common one is humiliation on the part of the guy. There is a huge shame factor involved in your wife sleeping with another man. Being turned on by the shame and humiliation felt seems to be very common with cucks.

It is common that the cuck enjoys being told about or witnessing the wife with a man whose cock is substantially bigger. Someone who makes her cum harder or more often. If this is true for you, the wife can often intensify these feelings by vocalizing her increased pleasure with another man. Even subtle things like, "God his cock feels so damn good." can make the cuck feel like she means it feels better than his in a way he enjoys.

Pegging is another common one. Pegging is a woman fucking a man's ass with a strap-on or similar toy for those of you unfamiliar with the term. Pegging has seen a huge shift lately becoming more and more common with straight men. Anal for both men and women has had a stigma of being taboo. It is quite literally dirty and messy. However, it feels good. It seems nowadays most couples have tried the man fucking the woman's ass. It is tighter for the guy and if the woman can relax, once the initial discomfort is over, it feels really good. There is also an element of submission involved. Most men feel dominate when taking a woman's ass. The tables are being turned more and more often. A man's prostate can only be reached through anal play so most men who try some form of anal play end up liking it. Couples commonly start small with the woman using a finger to stimulate the prostate when the man is having an orgasm. It makes the orgasm more intense. Couples often graduate to using a dildo or strap-on. This flips the role of the partners quite literally. The woman feels powerful and in control because she is the one doing the fucking for a change. The man feels submissive because he is the one getting fucked. Some couples take this to the point of the bull fucking the husband. Usually the bull is the one doing the fucking whether he is fucking a mouth or an ass, the women or the husband. Some couples love the idea of sharing the bulls cock.

Chastity is another common one you will see in cuck porn. The woman uses a chastity device to prevent the man from getting an erection. This is also a play on turning the roles. The woman is in complete control on whether or not the man can reach orgasm. Usually sex ends when the man reaches orgasm, even if the woman hasn't. There are couple that play with chastity in the short term, just putting on the device for an hour or two for a play session. There are also couples that enjoy long term chastity where the device is locked on and the woman keeps the key. This ensures the man cannot masturbate when the woman isn't around. Some couples also do prostate milking as part of the chastity play. This is when the man is denied orgasm for at least a week or two. The woman then pegs him or uses a toy or her fingers to massage his prostate. This will cause him to expel semen without feeling an orgasm or without even being erect. This obviously makes the man feel extremely submissive because she is taking complete control of his body and forcing him to ejaculate without orgasm. It will be a slower drip than an orgasm though.

Feminization/forced fem/sissification is another common fetish. This involved the husband dressing and/or acting more feminine. You have probably seen cuck porn where the husband is dressed in a slutty maid outfit with a chastity device on. This is a common theme. This is usually about making the cuck feel like less of a man, especially in contrast to the bull. There is a wide spectrum here and since it is something that Greg isn't into, we have limited experience with it firsthand.

BBC or Big Black Cock is a common theme in porn. The cuck watching his wife with a black man who is substantially bigger than him is a fetish for some. This ties into the humiliation of knowing the bull is much larger and therefore is pleasing her more than the cuck ever could.

Another thing you will see in porn is the cuck eating the creampie or cum out of his wife after the bull fucks her. You might see the "reluctant" cuck who is totally hesitant to do so. Or you will see the sissy cuck who enjoys it. This might also include the cuck licking the taste of his wife off the bull's cock. This might happen in a couple where the cuck has bi tendencies. It might also happen with a cuck who isn't turned on by the bull, but the humiliation of it all.

Kat reacts: I am much more open to just about any kinks than Greg so I'm more comfortable with everything we talked about here. I will say that I think every guy should experience pegging at least once. Regardless of what your relationship is like and what fetishes/kinks you are into, it's worth trying. The main reason for this is it will show you what it feels like to get fucked. It is an eye-opening experience. Just like any dominate should try being submissive or vice-versa. A healthy relationship should include trying to understand your partner as much as possible so that you can empathize with them better. A mindset of not asking your partner to do anything that you aren't even willing to try once is a good thing.

Greg reacts: Ok, now we've made it to cuckold territory. Listen up guys. We're not hot wifing anymore so nothing you say or feel fucking matter now. First word of advice. Don't touch the bull while he's doing his business. Hands off. Nothing will make a straight man's cock go limp like getting touched by another guy. Your wife will hate you for it so you better be a good little sub and behave. The only thing you need to worry about is making sure that your wife and bull are comfortable, which usually involves just doing what the fuck they say.

I don't have much to say about the fetishes, they are what they are and I've tried them all.

Solving Problems

There are a lot of problems that can come up along the way and we have already discussed them a bit. During the beginning of the transition the big thing is getting on the same page. If you are openly talking about this the whole way then it will be a bit easier. But there will still be points along the way when you are not on the same page and it will cause tension.

Maybe the wife is totally opposed to the idea at first. Hopefully you are going slowly in the process and not wanting to bring it up and have her in a threesome that weekend. For some women, they will be willing to go fast, but it is more common that you need to move slowly. If either one of you pushes too hard and it causes a conflict, the best thing to do is to back down for a little while. Let the seed of the idea just sit in your partners mind and don't push it again for a while.

Think of this process just like any major change in your life and marriage. If you want to move to a different state, for example, it is going to be a slow thing. You aren't going to wake up one day and tell your spouse you want to move out of the blue and expect them to start packing. It is something that requires a lot of conversations and patience.

Final Thoughts

The big picture here is that this lifestyle and the progression into it is different for every couple. How you got to the point of reading this book and where you go from here is entirely up to you. There is no right or wrong way to do this. What matters is that you are both happy with the arrangement and are having fun! The internet makes it easy to find people who share your interest in this. Reach out and make some friends that are also in the lifestyle that you can talk to! I'm not going to mention any specific websites because this book isn't an ad, just our thoughts and experiences to hopefully help!

Made in the USA
Thornton, CO
03/15/25 19:26:18

627d7172-b28d-435b-a053-94228d9f0627R01